ZERO GRAVITY FUNK LIBIDO

by David Hurlin

BLUE LIGHT PRESS ❖ 1ST WORLD PUBLISHING

1ST WORLD
PUBLISHING

SAN FRANCISCO ❖ FAIRFIELD ❖ DELHI

Winner of the 2019 Blue Light Book Award
Zero Gravity Funk Libido

BLUE LIGHT PRESS
www.bluelightpress.com
bluelightpress@aol.com

1ST WORLD PUBLISHING
PO Box 2211
Fairfield, Iowa 52556
www.1stworldpublishing.com

BOOK DESIGN
Melanie Gendron
melaniegendron999@gmail.com

COVER ART
Sarah Matzke

COVER DESIGN
George Foster

AUTHOR PHOTO
Ryan Koch Photography

FIRST EDITION

Library of Congress Control Number: 2019951626

ISBN: 9781421836423

ACKNOWLEDGMENTS AND APPRECIATION

I am grateful to family, friends, mentors and writers who have helped me give birth to this book.

I would like to thank my uncle, Dan Hurlin, who gave me a copy of *Howl* when I was a teenager. It was the first poetry book that I owned, it gave me permission for everything.

I am grateful to my uncle Peter Davis for his thorough feedback, encouragement, and support. I would have been far for the worse without his irreverent mentorship, book recommendations, and orange sherbert-fueled philosophy-Red Sox-laughing sessions.

Extra special thanks to Diane Frank for her guidance, her fearlessness as a writer, editor, and musician, and for ceaselessly empowering other writers. Her workshop feedback and her life, by example, were instrumental in these poems finding their true depth and vision.

Thank you to my wife, Emily Wofford, for her constant light, love, grace and elegance, and for her unconditional support of my music and writing, no matter the place or time. Thank you for your devotion and for your humbling and scintillating intelligence. The feeling of being with you is what it feels like to be home. I love you.

Thank you to my mom, Helen Davis, for creating a deep sense of safety and freedom in regards to self-expression; to my dad, Bill Hurlin, for passing down his love of reading and art; to my brother Eric Hurlin, for being the living representation of all that I strive for in art and life and who had the courage to cold call Russell Edson from a Friendly's diner in Darien to invite him out for ice cream; to my son, Dil Hurlin, for his powerful mind, his wild sense of humor, and for always inspiring me with his drawings and music, his untamed, brilliant and creative life.

Thanks to the rest of my named and unnamed art-sound-music-writing-love-life community:

Blue Light Press, 1ˢᵗ World Publishing, Monday Night Poets, Rustin Larson, Robin Lim, Brett Maddux, Edmund Miller, James Singleton, Melanie Gendron, George Foster, Sarah Matzke, Ryan Koch, James Moore, Elizabeth Moen, Gemma Cohen, Jonnie Cohen, Dan Padley, Dana T, Mike Dillon, Richard Beymer, Anna Gebhardt, Nicholas Naoti, Monserrat Iniguez, Nynke Passi, Christine Schrum, Erich Martin, Natalia Danel, Ben Foster, Zac Sluser, Jonathan Lynch, Anup & Anita Ghosh, Gillian Brown, Gyan Shrosbree, Juli Crockett, Joule L'Adara, Timothy Donnelly, Dom and Phil Rabelais, Jennymay Wardwell, Ben Davis, Nick Davis, Dirty Gerund Poetry, Flat Black Studios, Stanton Moore Drum Academy, Cody Olivas, Taylor Ross, Matt Reischling, Shannon Kring, Ben Daniels, Steve Giacomini, Tim Britton, and so many more I love. I am grateful for you all.

Grateful acknowledgment to the following anthologies in which some of these poems were accepted for publication: *River of Earth and Sky: Poems for the 21st Century* (Blue Light Press, 2015), *Jellyfish* (Boathouse Press, 2002).

for Peter Clement Davis (1939-2010)

TABLE OF CONTENTS

COURTESY AT THE THEATER

"Excuse me, please," is the natural thing to say when having to disturb anyone in order to get to or leave your seat in a theater, and if someone is obliged to get up to let you pass, you add, "Thank you" or "I'm sorry." When climbing in and out of a row of seats, face the stage or front and press closely to the backs of the seats you are facing, being careful not to drag your coat or purse over the heads of those seated in front of or behind you.

— *Emily Post's Etiquette*, "Courtesy at the Theater."

"Excuse me, please,"
    may I touch your hair?
    The dark moon oar of your long Indian hair?
    or better yet when you are getting
    some Milk Duds before the snack bar closes,
    will you brush up against me?
    Drag your umbrella of hair
    across the desert of my neck?

"Excuse me, please,"
    may I turn you into light?

"Excuse me, please,"
    will you be my hovercraft?

"Excuse me, please,"
    may we spiral in the nudity of reality?

"Excuse me, please,"
    can we gyroscope in the guts of a dream?

"Excuse me, please,"
    May we share this seat
    hidden in the shadows of the projection

light? May we privately intertwine,
secretly hold the lips
of our hands together?

"Excuse me, please,"
	May we levitate now? I'm ready to writhe
	in the white public of midair,
	to cover your skin with nocturnal balm
	to make the collaborative shadow puppet
	of our dance bark on the blue horizon.

"Thank you,"
	stranger for sitting here in giant warmth
	with me for the last two hours.

"Thank you,"
	for sharing your coat and,

"I'm sorry,"
	but tonight is the night that I die
	the way I always wanted to,
	during a rainstorm. Your hair
	is the black ocean of the shipwreck.
	Rose-slit bindi, cusp of lightning
	that is your entire body.
	I am the captain trapped at sea
	in the quiet freedom of surrender,
	in between the guillotines of razor light,
	who has just realized he must
	go down with the ship.

EDEN

Her Venus flytrap earrings are hungry.
The ghost of Salvador Dali
applies her makeup with a flamethrower.
A burning avalanche of blush
that almost rips the skin off
while his pet jaguar paces back and forth
in front of the bedroom door.
Her skin, like a double exposure
of a Venezuelan waterfall
and the red curtain that hangs
in the butcher shop.
The roaring of blood
as it pounds
rock into sand
underwater.
Meat hooks swaying
like clock pendulums
from her rib cage.
Gymnastics rings
over a smoking caldera
in the Voodoo kitchen
of her ancestors.
A Gauguin tiger curled up and licking
dinner blood from her hair.
She is dressed like a car accident
with the Post-Impressionist
Photoshop filter applied.
Dark earth metals,
ribbons pulled unwillingly
from the volcano,
and strangler fig trees

from the surrounding jungle
are forged together and made
into a gown for her
with blacksmith hammers
and a diamond blade saw.
Incarnation of the color scarlet,
she walks into the room
like a chain reaction,
a Paparazzi detonation
for the premiere of a film
in which she stars
as the *accident prone girl*
who has been able to change
the weather with her mind
since she was a child.
The hidden fault line
has opened like a tongue,
a red carpet of lava
for her to walk barefoot on
like the Hindu bride, Sita,
forced to prove her chastity
by fire.

CLOSING TIME AT CAFE PARADISO

The tables and chairs seem
to have their own agendas.
Placed like bad installation art
or the really hard level of a video game
where you must jump
from stone to impossible stone
to avoid death by lava.

Ceiling fans turn at two tempos
while the coinage is counted at the counter
panned left in the psychoacoustic architecture
of your skull receiving espresso,
facing the twilight traffic of two roads
through the wall-sized windows.

B.B. King hasn't started playing yet
but the samba has dissolved into a piano ballad for now.
Gold mouth of the saxophone, open
like a koi fish breathing, navigating
the tight circle of a dark pond
in the lobby of a Chinese restaurant.

A chair is dragged across the tile floor by the door
and an accidental harmony is struck with the sax.
Screeching-bent-timespace-chord
from two wildly unconnected realms,
over the hum of disconnected conversations,
those unintelligible exchanges between sentient beings
who have inexplicably congregated
to drink coffee on a dark winter afternoon.

All these life stories blend together.
Some amateur witch's brew-
squirrel-broth-stew, the winter's antidote
served freely in the soup kitchen of the God damned
beautiful, while the temperatures continue to soar
below zero, with wind chills so cold, you start to realize
you have risked everything for this.

FALSE VACUUM STATE

Hot air balloon
like a testicle stapled
to the carnival dart booth
wall of a dull July sky.

Sun dragging its empty cans west.
Clover in the grass like whiteheads.
A brick.

An unvarnished bird claps
across the field in a recoil
of self-thrown UFO landing wind
that bends the grass.

Hill.
Red pickup truck;
keys in the ignition.
Gas cans in the back
like schoolgirls.

Clouds.
Smokestack
in a hot blue haze.

One ant
an inch from the outer ring
of an ant hole.

And the possibility
that somewhere in outer space
enough energy has been generated
to knock a possibly false vacuum state

into a true vacuum state
which would set off
a sphere of annihilation
that would grow invisibly
at the speed of light
in all directions
from the spark of origin
destroying everything as it blooms
so completely that the basic laws
of physics would erase
resulting in the end
of the universe.

APOCALYPSE EXIT STRATEGY

The end of a poem
as a metaphor for death
is probably a bad idea.

The idea of the end
as a new beginning
is bad too, like when

you go to the movies
and you know that what
you have seen is

just an advertisement
for the sequel
next Thanksgiving.

Orgasm is a bad choice
too, the rocking mobile
of the solar system

on the low ceiling
in the yellow shadows
of the Christmas lights.

As if making love
could actually hold a candle
to death.

As if self-destruction
could simplify the map
to the buried city.

Apocalypse is a bad choice
and almost all my poems
end with the apocalypse,

as a metaphor for sex,
death, and new beginnings
all at once.

The apocalypse exit strategy
is a quadruple sin of literature.
Worse than airport prices.

There might be a way.
The delicate and almost
imperceptible haunting

of the suicide pilot,
realizing he would rather live
running in the mountains.

KALI

for Seema

Badminton racket hissing in the summer air.
The familiar twang of contact
like a Mexican love song played
at 108 times normal speed
so it's over as it's begun
while lace birdies fly into my mouth
barefoot on a field of clover.

I am afraid of losing you.
If I lost you right now
I would only survive because
my skin still smells like you.
My bones are still warm
from our double candle of sleep,
interrupted only once by a fire alarm
at 3:17 AM.

Sometimes it pisses me off
how you can maintain your life perfectly
while I get shipwrecked between your legs
and wake up in your room
just as you are leaving
having already walked through
a vanished curtain of spray perfume,
telling me you love me,
with those Sharpie cuts of eyeliner,
and rusted rose lipstick,
to kiss me like a daughter would
her dead father.
My eyes, brier patches
of clawed veins like sea plants

or nebulae over-lit and revolving
in their display cases.

I have lost to the recoil of the night again.
I lie in bed a malfunction of the catapult.
Shocked by my apathy.
Shocked by my tears.
But not at all surprised
by the sacred violence
that I have worshiped your body with,
like a bullet turned into a parachute
butterfly knife of hair opening
down the runway of your back.
I feel like vomiting or singing
something to let the frozen ground know
about your eyes held in tears,
the lines of your mouth
the memorization of your back
the gravity of your nipples
making sand carvings in my chest
the helicopter landing pad of your breast plate
for my right hand,
and the thousand helping hands
on the thousand armed goddess chopper pilot
of your heart
in a mismatched marriage between a word
and its forms.

I know you are beautiful
and it will remain a secret forever,
esoteric even to you.

ZERO GRAVITY FUNK LIBIDO

I like to get wild when I surf
the Internet. Simple post-midnight pleasures.
Thirty seconds ago I searched for
"zero gravity funk libido"
to see if it would generate
any responses. Zero.

I plugged in our band name,
"The Apocalypso Tantric Boys Choir of Memphis"
to see if we had made it
into the entertainment section
on some local website. Or unknowingly
into a virtual calypso newsletter
with international readership.
Perhaps an article by a ranting critic
violently disappointed that the boys choir,
contrary to her fiery expectations,
had played a four-hour non-stop set
of avant-garde funk.

I am going search for
"Her mango eyes
brighter than the sun
at the bottom of the ocean,
blue bandanna pulled parallel
with her perfect eyebrows,
raised like lightning,
the kind of cobras
that come as premonitions
of the final test of enlightenment,
hovering like sex itself,
tilting down the sun

roof, sticking her head out,
soft lips and long black hair
while the engine runs
for at least twenty minutes
in the parking lot,
dropping her off staring,
considering to wish
that I was black, ripped,
loaded, emotionally stable,
indifferent to poetry and jazz,
completely over my last relationship,
and capable of handling how much I like
this gorgeous 21-year-old Indian woman
that I will never be with,
from the Italian neighborhood
in Queens, New York,
savoring the dark chocolate fact
that she wants to get ice cream
with me some time, and share
the Reese's Peanut Butter Cups
that I bought for her
just after half-filling the tank
at the BP Station on Second Street
in Fairfield, Iowa,
United States of America,
just before 5:30 PM
on a gorgeous May 22nd, 2002."

BAGEL

Working behind the counter
at Einstein Bagels in Chicago
she has smirk eyes
and flirt breasts.
She is tiny with mantis limbs
and sideways eyes, big
round bagel holes,
moose head eyes.
She is Mexican
and smiles at me
like it's not allowed
she is a deer in headlights
content with public submission.
A secret, a closed book
with a padlock, sexy
as purgatory
but slightly mal-
nourished, thin as a dart
in a bulls eye
coat hanger veins,
hair in a ponytail
pulled through the hole
in her over-sized job hat.
I bet she looks incredible
in a red dress,
and loud shoes
or in baggy sweat pants
after work.

When I was ordering
I didn't see her naked
but now I do

mounted like a hood ornament
on the hard gloss of her lover.
I am the voyeur
the bullshit artist
making her hair wet,
raspberry cream cheese
on her nipples
which he licks off
as her back bends
against the five PM light,
her hat on the floor
he rips her with love
and a parachute opens
inside of her.

They are having one
of those parachute weddings
in the nude
the rush of wind up their spines,
goosebumps like thorns.
He clicks into her
like a piece of toast
her soft lips gently slit
with the auratic gleam
of her perfect teeth,
her eyeballs rolled back
like satellite dishes
taking the universe
into their small bowls.

They are lovers,
his butt clenches like a heart
his feet are sweating
beads of sweat condensing
his thighs are tight

and their breathing
tears down the sidewalk
from Lake Michigan.
She's on top of him
like a spiral staircase
working her small body
on top of his,
straddling his hourglass
working him like a sailboat
paintbrush joystick
her breasts barely bounce
because they're so hard
like moon rocks.

BRUNCH

Scrambled eggs used as a face mask
by the grave robber dressed in black,
bearded, with melted cheese for hair,
albino goat-wig drip
and a six foot long spork,
oiled for the unholy excavation.
Leaving the plate, the choreography
of the inanimate begins,
the voyeur-zoom into brunch,
omelet levitation–
the yellow cloud in the mirror
suspended by fishing wires
like hairline fractures in the sky,
paper cuts all the way to the sun.
Marionette swaying like an undead hog
hooked to a frosted log chain and half disappearing
in the freezer fog,
digging as the pendulum digs through sand magenta,
hissing erosion of the dune into Lake Michigan,
the bridge crumbling as you run falling,
the Noah's Ark reenactment in the stomach,
ventricle floodwater and acid rain.
Pink ultrasound of the elephant, weightless,
sphere of xerox light, the glowing edges
where the crib is buried in the ground.
Preman rib cage polished with toothbrushes
safety slats blossoming naked through the dirt
the bed as a prison rising now by service elevator
sporklifted.
The trough of ghost pepper hot sauce
like Satan's crowfoot bathtub
for the grave robber to dunk his steaming head in

and then run like hell without spilling the mimosas
through the gossiping forest
back to the black getaway van
parked behind the old Wal-Mart.

THE HEART

is a fetus
in a crib of rib cage.
A stalactite
that has dripped itself
all the way to the floor
and is growing wide.
Ice trunk lighthouse ooze.
Dark juice commander.
Avatar on a meat hook.
Stigmata headquarters
with five umbilical cords
emptying out into the night
on mermaid-fiber optic octopus arms,
suspending the spider's brain,
the grotesque engine
of primal wetness
with its boomerang blood
cockpit and pendulum.
Naked pet.
Half nightwatchman.
Half night.

ODE TO THE REMOTE CONTROL HELICOPTER SALESMAN AT THE CENTURY CITY MALL

His burden
weightless.
Futurist hawk master
in a revelation
of toy aviation,
the sensationless ascension
into the Uncreated Flame,
like a cinematic reverse
of the *Titanic*.

Leonardo DiCaprio
swimming toward the lens
to kiss you on the lips
while you shiver on a floating door
flying back now
to its naked hinge
in the bedroom.

A dandelion
or an orange butterfly
blooming out the eye hole
of a skull.

A wedding dress
hitting the bed
while the Brâncuși
it has fallen from melts
into the diamond tomb
of a lion-claw tub.

Fifty billion golden
retrievers retrieving
the same stick.

Robbie Madison
jumping over a football field
on his dirt bike
to break the Guinness Book
World record.

Umbrella of dynamited roses
from the dunk crux
of the John McCracken launch pad
into the illuminated darkness
of the unknown!

Those tiny lights
the bejeweled pharaoh
of physics,
in the camouflage
of stars, off
to save lives.

BIG DIPPER STILL LIFE

Tonight the Big Dipper stands on its handle
like a horse on its back legs.

Not frightened by a rifle or a rattlesnake
but silent with black majesty, pulled back,

and flat against the sky like a Ferrari logo,
arrested in the ice-void of vertigo on the horizon.

The snapshot freeze of the butcher knife.
The swing set zenith of terrible emptiness.

The Milky Way all the way here, to the still life
that I interrupt by existing.

Rug. Mint green guitar, off-set, pointing
like a compass to the box-spring.

The glass bull illuminated on a pile of ATM slips.
The sleeping laptop, black and open, and this

pad of newsprint like an oversized guestbook,
for me to write my name, address, and comments

to the owner about how nice the people are,
the incredible food, and the seven star view.

PRAYER TO THE LIGHTNING GOD
PART I

Each leaf that falls is a death.
A blossom of electric forehead ash.
Towering walls of trees
that run the river green.
Purring machine of death.
White noise ovation
of clapping on the other side,
white flag of incinerated saints
marching through the walls with death sutras.
The wind-sucking gills of God.
Veins reins of golden flesh
pouring the Des Moines outward.
Every ripple is its own annihilation.
The hawk with memories of ancestors
in his soaring bones
flying through the white tunnel
and the hunted fleeing
in the ecstasy of fear.
That thread of slime
that runs through all incarnations
binding the generations in perpetual flight.
An avalanche of feathers and skulls
steering the metal canoe,
a snake pulled
by the weight of the water
towards the lowest point.
Each molecule,
an ant under a magnifying glass,
in a colossal Lego mosaic
made with devotion to the lightning God.
Hearts flashing plastic Pandora cracks.

Book ash urn clasp broken and radiating
flashlit dust from the keyhole
a solitary ray of sunlight
in a deserted factory.
The path of the wound
metallic and immortal,
like a gray hair pulled slowly
out of a mouthful of caesar salad.

NINE IRON

I think of you now the way I imagine
lightning before it destroys,
droning quietly in the electric purple
chest of a thunderhead.

I am the suicidal idiot
revving the chopper engine
of a hideous romance,
standing in the turquoise shallow end
of a rooftop swimming pool,

shivering in the dry storm winds
nipples harder than life,
shamelessly waving a nine iron
at the silver tower of sky.

I stand here now in a white towel
on a Saturday night, still dripping
after my long hot shower because
I purposefully didn't dry off
before writing all of this down,

thinking the inclusion of the authentic
image of me dripping and almost naked
in a black doorway of steam, would emphasize
the full charge of this poem,

crashing through the trap door of heaven
on a wrecking ball
to split open this white page
with the entire darkness of the sky.

ODE TO THE ABSURD

You can feel a poem
come in like an intruder,
standing at the self-checkout
kiosk in Wal-Mart, singing
pseudo gospel in your head
while you buy Mexican beer
after midnight on the darkest night
in 500 years.

Thinking of Camus and absurdity
as you walk back to your car
Sisyphean, laughing out loud
at astronomy compared to beer
and the commodification of *survival*.

Trying to decide how to deal with this intrusion,
whether to lean toward autobiography
or baby wizard logic,
the delicious mix
of delusion and faith,
the ridiculous optimism
that you could befriend the bear
loose in your neighborhood
if worst comes to worst.

That state of mind
where the elements become aphrodisiacs.
Fire licking the bricks.
Water lapping the dock.
Air howling in the dark corridors.

Or that place where the two intersect,

the light on the front porch
that comes on when you know
someone you love is coming over to visit.

The linen closet
that leads to the jungle.

The garage
with a time machine in it.

The Cedar View Bridge
carried to Canada by eagles.

The pillow for the golden bowl
of the skull to receive an offering
from Netflix.

HOW TO WATCH TELEVISION

for Timothy

1. Turn on the television.

2. Position yourself on the couch facing the television.

3. Open the silver bowl of your brain to receive the blue electrons of air, like see-through blueberries from another planet or dimension. Crushed by alien or angel feet, the toe sauce to make wine for the poison. Reach for the zebra blanket of sparking static and polyester partial suffocation, like fish paper folded around neon salmon wrapping your AI dreamscape, spelunking through your third eye like the twisted smoke of incense. The iconography has changed. The halo is a rectangle and Jesus has been crowned with Easy Cheese. The minimalism of the true altar becoming woke and agitated two-way mirrors, drone blood, zero gravity furniture parade painting the ceiling with sea foam, spewing out the cracks like a 360 degree waterfall. Eyeball retinas fish-hooked by narrative, the sunken jewels of Bluetooth pirates drooling their arms into the mouths of sparkling caves. Mermaid diadems, fancy fangs the boiling breast milk shivering the wakes of night ships stealing the cargo of deep freeze electrons from your silver bowl of liquid nitrogen, smoking as you are in the morning when you are awake but you can't move your body yet. The bed holding you hostage as the square sun billboards you like full frontal nudity. Tempur-Pedic iron maiden. Xmas straight jacket. Fake tan skull puppet, zip-tied to the headboard like a headless goat at the petting zoo, walking in circles. Firepit and the pendulum zeroing in on the kiss of the diamond blade, the circular saw moaning in the star factory where light is a captive of the future.

CASTLE OF LOVE

for Emily

Over time I've been building
my castle of love
through the starry spider groin.
Hear the standing ovation
for the sun
in the heaving leaves.
I see you bird squawker.
I smell where your monologue
meets the sky spinning green.
Oh tornado, funnel of ball bearings
and shark light
reaching down to touch Texas
inspiring awe effortlessly
like the vacuum salesman
ceaselessly pulling swatches of dirt
from under our couch cushions
for the wife archetype in both of us
in the *calling child services*
dirty sections of the archaeology
of our future couch fire
layers of popcorn, dog hair,
and the toxic shock of watching
Breaking Bad again holding each other
in between Sea Salt & Vinegar kisses
and foot massages with the same oil
we cook with
as we watch unspeakable acts of violence and insanity
in the same manner we would watch a sunset
and with the same amount of pleasure
two evil spirits in love
illuminated blue by the pain, cries,
suffering and anguish of others
like gods, we sit
and do nothing.

NEBRASKAN DAYMARE

Yes but can you soften
and drop the silk rope
humming through the groove
into the endless well of black
walnut ink you never made?

Can you hold still long enough
for the leaves Lilliput, to start tying you up
as you lie drowsy from the breathing
percussion of light and leaves
tied together by sound?

Can you lengthen and adjust
your parallel lines, oh kissing mirrors,
to hover burning infinite, like a filament,
solitary flashlit steel string
tuned to the North Star?

Spring-muscled dandelion flying machines
like UFOs painted from the inside with daylight.
Oh Daymare Supreme!
Can you encircle the naked waist
with only one arm?

Can you spread your pink petals
out on the glass table
like the folded map of Nebraska
that gets wrecked in the rain
when you open it?

SCENIC OVERLOOK

Highway drone in the silent
machinery of the blossom, the way
the forest folds into smoking
snow and melts in the air, almost mist,
the weightless ash, sideways confetti
of the apocalypse, the scrolling codes,
all the torrential unraveling, crumbling
of ones and zeros, keys
and keyholes, zoo lightning.
Zeus-mudra shadow puppetry
against the drum-stretched retinas,
the antler-lock of kissing pelvii
next to the scenic overlook sign
where the charred-black landscape marks
the indisputable end of tourism.
When, after all the water is gone,
the camera becomes medieval
and the tour guide is bound,
bludgeoned to death and eaten,
his remains, a decomposing strobe-
lit, post-erotic carcass
that stinks of extinction, of burning
flesh, as foul as breath itself.
Moth flitting against the hanging lantern,
flag yolked cold to the spine,
that swaying of the dock
and the lake, swaying
of the pendulum within,
the yellow claw of the hinge
digging through the heart
of the mountain for a tunnel.

REAL ESTATE DEVELOPMENT

It's possible for one person
to be an entire synchronized
swimming team unto themselves.
Undulating mandalas
of slippery flesh tied
into the sunken nest docket.
The pubic hair rising
against the draining bathtub
mirror, cyclone
into the translucent navel.
Floodlights of the yellow crane
the shivering 1/2 ton arm
into the stomach, the clench
of raining dirt to make room
for the swimming pool.

Oh! Oh! Oh! Pummel
my sweet piggy bank slot,
siphon the river of twisting milk
into the kamandalu-Jack
O' Lantern fire licking
the twin rock-cut cliffs
between my crumbling legs
of limestone, these gilded snakes
leaving emblazoned maps of skin
for you to find, intricate replicas,
soul luggage unzipped, the ghost
alphabet echoing in the sand.
Breadcrumbs on a beach of diamonds
for all you little witch doctors
working on your first cure.

UNTITLED

When I breath in with my ear
pressed to the bicep vein
I hear the howling
of an empty farmhouse
an ancient hinge
creaking on a dark axis
cicada shell-powder snowing like sparks
in the boo-hiss blooming
of the welder helmet glass
during the formation of a planet

BUFFALO STAMPEDE THROUGH THE ZODIAC

Smithereen powder
sheet of Jupiter dust,
a sweeping sail
on the hellbent horizon.
Double-kick ventricle pump
of hooves like beetles
the size of cow eyes.
Seven story brick wall
knocked down and rolling
on the backs of fire ants,
crushing hill greens
in an avalanche
of buckeye fossil turds
cramming through the chest pipe,
the hourglass hole,
planted with a camouflage abatis
of alligator teeth and fingernails.
The enwreathed arm wrestle of horns,
a black grate of brier patch
in a lip-lock of electric gloss
gutting the barracuda
from the dock pile.
Drilling its permanent helix
of snow shovels
through the wet innards,
the necks of a thousand
ostriches braided together
into a weed whacking crown
of beaks turning sand carvings
into 360 degree rainbows
of pulverized glass
like spilt slug salt,

the explosion of the sun
or a rock dropped in a pond of skin
devoured by the solitary body
of a million eels in a cold spot,
packed tight with feathers
hooves and horns into a telescope
shoved deep into your third eye
that makes your dark frog skin
shiver while the cyclops of night
enters you like floodwater.

TYPHOON BUTTERFLY

I lie on my chin in the green light
of my digital clock
balancing a bowling pin in a dream.
The silence is magnetic,
buzzing electric
like waiting for the first song
to start on a new album,
spinning like an idling flying saucer.

I think to myself
maybe God turned on his PA system
to make an announcement
but then decided against it.
So I roll over in bed
a little disappointed
as if the new album never started playing.

I throw my blankets
against the wall as a hard as I can
and a sheet corner snaps me in the eye
like the butterfly who starts
a 2 mile wide typhoon in Miami.
The incense smoke sways a little to the left.
The cinder block wall ripples into the sky
like Jacob's ladder
and the stars with their muscle of light
dump a five gallon bucket
of iced Fruit Punch Gatorade
on God's head.

THE GREAT WHEEL

The tire blew out
when we were fighting
about other women.
The van spent two nights
on the shoulder of 215 South
across from the Air Force base
where nuclear weapons
are stored underground.

Three days later
an enormous tow truck-driving angel
speaking walkie-talkie Spanish
picks me and my van up
and takes us to the tire shop.

It's like a Venn diagram
of purgatory and salvation.
I feel like the Virgin Mary
riding sidesaddle on her donkey
to the tire-stacked manger
with a bionic Joseph and bouncer.

The grease-blown bucktooth mechanic
greets me with an air-powered socket gun
and a silver hammer
to break off my useless dealership lugs
to be replaced with solid metal ones.

A five pentacle star in the hubcap,
the wheel of fortune,
the relentless cycle of life and death.

Northbound.
Southbound.

At the tire shop,
I feel that I'm at the silent center
of the Great Wheel.
Other people's lives are in full force,
burning up the highways of the world.
The oceans crushing shells into sand.
Corpses getting their faces made up,
the women moaning
the terrible joys of childbirth,

but I'm just barely sitting here,
listening to the crows interact
with the adrenal bristling of power tools.
I know that somehow I am beyond
all of these mundane theatrics.
I'm not even in sync with the slower pace of the hawk above,
or that of the orange echelons of mountains
or the flat line of the desert
parking lot. I refuse even to be myself today
and the current age carries on without me.

THE YOGA OF TELEKINESIS

There are scissors on the sink
and you try to lift them with your mind.
Qigong wet dream. The hovering
white plank of energy to summon

the vacuum of psychic muscle
needed to suspend a pair of scissors
in front of the bathroom mirror,
midair.

Arms tense like there is a great undertaking,
a great stabilization, a beach ball
being pushed to the bottom
of the ocean with one arm.

Every cinematic cliché and visualization
about what it would take
to lift an object
with willpower alone.

As if God slammed the pin into the forearm
of your tiny Voodoo doll,
just violent enough for you to break
out of the handcuffs of gravity.

The instinct to summon all your might
for some Herculean ghost-clench,
the sardine of the third eye
exploding in the microwave.

Seismic tremors of the hands
like Parkinson's, accelerating

piano crescendo, the bent shape of your consciousness
catalyst of the invisible blossom

a wild yellow eye
opening in the paw
of a tiger, the claw of the eagle
unzipping rainbow trout from the river.

Shaking arms of missionary Tantra,
pushing a car stuck in the snow,
pulling the head of Medusa
out of your carry on at airport security.

There is the assumption
of extreme human effort,
the same hunger for freedom
that the Icarian Sea is named after,

the desire to see flying scissors
as some sort of paranormal autograph
and yet in spite of this mind blowing exertion
you get the sense that the scissors

would only have the impulse
to obey your command,
to whisper into the sugar water of the mirror
like the iridescent posture of the hummingbird

if you spontaneously arrived
at the secret wizard sound by accident,
the primal sigh of relief,
the exhale of the willow by the river.

Such a complete and utter surrender
to the way things are exactly how they are

that as if by hammock,
weightlessness, occurs all by itself.

Ancient moorings of orbit,
scissors shining in the dark,
like a satellite silently calibrating
to new coordinates.

MARCH

Relentless whip-smash
     of cold sinks its hull one inch deeper
     into the moonscape.
When the skull empties into a room
     of haunted sounds, a Grecian dome,
     a train's black lineage pressing its code
     through a tunnel of wolf eyes.
When the backbone is subway tracks
     whispering with lethal voltage,
     the electric map under the city.
When the skull becomes an O'Keeffe
     the color of sunrise, time-lapse
     shadows of an absent brain.
When jack-in-the-box Venus
     is gnawing at his own springs
     covering the gnash-scented metal
     with Pavlovian saliva.
When the skull is a bubble blown
     with rainbow edges
     through the silent circle of my ear.
When the phone rings in every atom
     like sand on glass, refrigerator shiver,
     cuneiform, Rosetta stubble and resurrections.
When all the demons
     have ascended into the light
     and the Sharpie marker
     has exploded up there
     on the white cinder block wall
     and the tears unzip
     themselves, take down
     their ghost hair and fall
     to dissolve in Niagara Falls

slipping from my control
being pushed running downhill
back breaking into wings
that burn like eucalyptus
in the molecules of sunlight
that connect their soft joints
to the body and burn
like steam irons.
Then I find myself saying
into your left ear, your
navel, your vulva, your
mouth, your skin, your right
ear that I love you.

NIGHT WALK IN THE GOLDILOCKS ZONE

Shadow moves on the houses.
Shovel-cut tongue
of sidewalk through the snow,
like the silver thread of a mountain pass.
A ninja silence that happens only
when everything becomes an omen.
0 degrees, feels like minus 12.
The engines purring on the front lawn
of a white trash diorama.
Restless plastic wrapping
of an abandoned porch.
The bristles of the wolf
stand erect, involuntary,
braille scarification huddled
around the igloo fires
in the nipples.
A microcosmic bar code
embedded for survival, for constellations
stopping the breath until
the car passes. Until
the sun passes through
the rib cage of an elephant.
Until the door latches
and the coat can be taken
off like skin, like a body;
This Goldilocks zone-tadpole descendant,
avatar of the swung triplet,
born of howling blackness
into the ocean of fire
woven closed by the pericardium.
This double cathedral.
This crystal well bucket drop.

This sunken cockpit
that powers the terror that powers
the tyranny of muscles,
collective of twitching pyromaniacs
who have initiated the chain-reaction
of the breath
as it turns to smoke.

YELLOW NIGHT

Thirty nine degrees outside.
This snowless bowl of night
is my black playground.
My own empty racetrack.
My neon love massacre.

Tonight is a subwoofer
sitting heavy like a pyramid
on my basement chest.

The yellow square
of this Post-it,
deep sky to drop
my burning coin into.
Parallel void of grill lights
on a semi-truck,
the foramen magnum gaping wide,
reflecting stars
in black ink.

Cymbals crash and echo
off the ancient walls.
Bass drum, toms, rewind.
Stomp my inner toms.
Crack my inner snare
like a glow stick.

Let's fuck hard tonight
so tomorrow morning
will feel like snow.

Dark yellow bulldozer

stopped in mid-dig.
Bright buildings.
Freezing glass.
A closed tanning salon.
Empty McDonald's parking lot
that I am writing in.
Yellow eye of Shiva
in the van ceiling,
fixed on a Post-it.
This leaf of grass,
throwing star of literature,
evidence of deep song.

Over 85 billion served
these first pages of winter.
This is a night to scream of love
the way a mother screams
when her child is walking
towards a busy street.
The kind of love
that saints burn with.
The kind of clarity
that surrounds the moon.

The highway glides silently
like a blue whale under the van
because the music is blasting.

Yellow no passing sign,
sideways pyramid,
gigantic reflective,
burning like a slice of Saturn cake
against the immaculate cold,
the sky, this holy night!

A night of saints and truckers
in Iowa. Its rusted palm barren
and bright with intrinsic fire.
This yellow night.

Old cassette tape rolling
the machinery of memory,
like the Des Moines River.
A moving sidewalk at O'Hare.
A tram up the Grand Teton.
A motorboat on Thorndike Pond.

Old cassette tape rolling,
squeaking, hissing, gliding heavy
like the Ocean City Ferris wheel,
lubricated pulley system,
Manhattan bound subway train,
wooden roller coaster dropping,
hands up in the church of night,
singing loudly these familiar drums,
and guitar punches. Rewinding
over and over this ferocious joy,
yellow cymbal crash of night.
Yellow night o' yellow night.

BARRACUDA

On a slow moving bicycle,
the white-haired child prodigy
is talking to himself
and shaking his head.
He passes by the windows
silently, like a barracuda
as the highway rumbles,
bending under the weight
of an eighteen wheeler.

ENLIGHTENMENT PART II

for Peter

Sometimes I feel It
like the bent consciousness
of an intruder in the living room.
I feel Its vertigo,
Its black presence.
I reach for my seven inch knife,
tip toe on the sea of white carpet,
and turn the doorknob slowly,
clinging to the floating
door of a shipwreck.

THE BEGINNING OF TIME

for Heather

Surrounded by drums and violent winds
I'm trying to get myself into a trance
so that I can write freely on the warm
rectangle face of a cardboard box
with the glue gun galaxy
where it was ripped open
to attain *Focaccia Cheese Bread.*

I sit alone on a dislocated minivan seat
in the garage, my walk-in closet
of pots and pans at midnight.

The best drum is in my lap;
it sounds the way a toaster oven glows.
Funky cattle brand pressing
orange snowflakes into the heart.

Rhythms, a tulip-bridge on fire
burning slowly back to the dark
shore where time started.
With my other hand, djembe
and conga hits work their chiropractics.

The cat, Medusa, sticks her head into a bowl
and chomps out a short solo while I feel
the ache of your king size bed
surrounded by open windows.

The wind is paranormal,
a shark, suspended like a god
in the dark green sky
of a glass aquarium,

or tearing past the garage
gathering its crazy weight
in exploding fields of popcorn,
to race trains and bend
everything capable of change.

Loose periwinkle sweat pants
blown to bone, like a moon flag,
on the side of the road for lilacs
to put behind my ear while I drum.
Where earlier, the police cars lit a blockade
for the hospital helicopter to take off
through the street-lit leaves,
falling upwards wind machine.

It was supposed to rain all day
but it wasn't until we got inside
that it started. Each molecule
in my body rained outwards
full double rainbows.
Front desk hotel operator
connecting me to my molecules
with bright colored patch cords.
My body became soft and wet,
sweaty and embarrassed
in the spotlight of an alien abduction,
gentle cleanse of rain
getting on the furniture,
grocery store mist machines
to bless the broccoli.
Trees and angels bent together
in worship of the storm
bright red war paint
dripping down my body
standing naked before you.

MANGER STAR

for Michael

Everyone's hearts are connected
by invisible strings
my mother once said
sitting on the edge of my bed.
Lights off, so I imagined
yellow-golden threads,
like spider silk in headlights,
shooting out in every direction
from my imaginary heart;
electric underwater plant,
Lion beams from the central source,
telephone wires carrying
spirits through copper tunnels.
Suspension bridges
of fiber optic ubiquity,
gleaming like the fishing wire
flying harness holding the weight,
during a zero gravity
Peter Pan song.

Tonight while I read
Michael McClure's
"Ode to a Negative Universe"
I remember all this.

I envision illuminated,
the specific thread
that connects my heart
to his heart, *rose-mammal.*
He is standing alone, in silhouette,
under the neon archway of a window

at the top of Coit Tower,
strumming an atonal nocturne
on his autoharp.

I wonder, but in my mind
I see, while I read his book *STAR*,
that he is glowing extra,
like kite fire, flaring yellow holy blue.
Like baby Jesus in the manger,
because my heart is opening,
the red circle of an ecstatic inhale,
because, in the gentle hours of the night
when my lover is sleeping,
our baby weightless
inside her voluptuous belly,
my ancient attention is his.

THE MUSIC OF MELTING

The page is open
like the yellow sky
of the apocalypse
reflected in the glass eye
of the gypsy ninja
whose RV is plugged
into the 220 jack
of my three prong heart.

I could tell by the way
you were sitting
playing with your hair
while you listened silently
on the second floor
that the lotus clutch
was unhitching
while the boom
extended its microphone
into the heart of the earth
to melt while recording
the music of melting.

I am killed by 24 karat gold
a monkey statue
pumping blood all night
in dark rivers of starlight
while the deer float
on the side of the road
in the fog of the mountain.

WHALE SONG

Sitting on a bench
in front of a demolished building
now covered in yellow grass.
A field of fire to fill
the ghostly rectangle
of the foundation.
The great smoothing is underway.
Race-car intelligentsia of the river
burning rock into light
to move among the mysteries
with the rainbow trout.
My body a river
sitting here crowned
with scars, samskaras, needing
smoothing, vinegar elixir
for the absence of heat
on this bench.
A spark trapped in a rock
listening to the crow
and the leaves conspire with the wind.
Breathing seam of red highway
soundtracking to the vanishing point.

North, the diamond tunnel of winter.
Train whistle like the song
of an unknown species,
a whale in an orange ocean of corn.
Scientists in the dark with headphones
transcribing their songs, harmonic love letters,
folktales from the sea floor,
the passionate histories of fishermen and pirates,
star farmers, ships, the swaying electricity

of the gulf-stream
incendiary barrier reefs
mirrored by the northern lights,
city lights on an alien horizon
the braille of a lucid romance,
some Christmas night walk
of another life, or another planet.
Standing together in the snow
the crystal smoke of our breathing
creating a single blossom
between our lips.

UNTITLED

I can hear the ocean
in your throat, in between kisses
your small mouth cupped to my ear
like the sky of an abduction.

VENUS TRANSIT

The problem with where
I am is that I am
in the middle of a love poem
soaring neon in the heart, the sun
last night, that nuclear
fulminating diorama
that sustains all life
on this planet
the exploding theater
for a very backlit
Venus transit. I watched
streaming video of NASA
coverage of the transit
the fleck of black paint
against the orange ping pong
ball bigger than a million earths.
The patient choreography
of the zodiac
and the corresponding psychological
ramifications, wild
gridlines of horoscope onto the brain
as into the abandoned
parking lot I stroll
as a floating deer
might stop to listen, I can
hear you, the kindness of your
heart, the expected miracle
of your arrival, deliberate and gorgeous
the turning that makes the sun rise.

TRASH DAY

I could see it. You are
Jesus Fucking Christ
with long red hair
and gorgeous vested tits
walking on an ocean of red
leaves in the fall, except you
are carrying a garbage bag
instead of your cross.

You are holy
in your vest
in your Jeep
in all your iconography.
Naked on top of me,
like a burning building,
your red hair curling
into black smoke, edged
by the star-white flesh
of your long narrow back.

Things near you hum
their true frequencies.
Even the trash must realize
its own perfect destiny
A yagya to Shakti,
an offering of melon rinds,
skittles wrappers, plastic
bags, Popsicle sticks, incense
ash, Kleenex, and a used up tube
of chapstick for the Garbage Truck
to crush in sacrificial fire.

I become a little boy around you
a warrior-king, a compassionate God-
drunk poet and a good kisser.
I become trash too.

All the parts of me
that need throwing out
are included in your embrace.
You inhale sunlight
exhale moonlight.

Just your silence makes me
pure, makes me sweat
in the breeze of your gait,
all gates open,

for the $600,000 horses
to race around the rings of Saturn

for the Jesus camels
to cross the deserts of Mars

for the squid choir
to rake the sands of Venus

for all the sunflowers
to lean toward the light
coming in through
the top of the garbage bag
on the side of the road.

SLOW DANCE ON HOT COALS

I still smell like smoke
from the fire pit last night.
Today the VHS blue of the sky
is erogenous-neon because the wind
is blasting the blue coals of heaven.
Branches scrape and lash
against the metal walls of our trailer
like skeletons, zombies
and robot-controlled mutant rats
trying to break in and steal my books,
my $700 snare drum,
my dreams and soul and wallet.

I offer you my heart
on a monolith of sunlight
straight from orange atoms.
A piece of grapefruit
with the sugar of biography,
holy crystals and rat poison.
It's an invitation to go crazy,
to pin the tail of the donkey
right on the crotch,
for the chasm of the underworld
to unsnap my bra, rip open my chest
and present a mirror of blood,
not so you can see what I have done
with my late nights and early mornings,
my slow dances on hot coals with Aphrodite.
Not so you can imagine the orange in my beard,
the African and Indian sunlight in my bones.

No. It's for you.

So you can be totally convinced
and know with certain knowledge
that the possums who fight in the woods
will eat you alive.

HEMISPHERES MAGAZINE ERASURE POEM

A raging fire destroyed everything. Time machine in the inferno our shredders of interior mathematics. The best highway, byways and Hawaiian diamonds to evoke images immaculate. Rosewater thousands luxuriating on a river of glass undiminished, unidirectional. Diver's house, floating in step with people and animals in plastic. Portable ballet engines, waiting for someone, photographing mirrors. What's emerging eccentric/musical claw-like drums. Men and women, custom instruments with lungs, nonstop subsidiaries, unmistakable true art iota. Then a message goes out, existential, hearing the call in the heart. Circles, your entire eye, minimal areas with signage. Dark evocative rock field lightest, strongest. Tuxedo black cathedral. Unlimited anthropomorphic wolves on racetracks, king Tut's tomb, headphones, seven sacred pools acoustic mapping, curse-reversing cities, cords relentlessly twisting river, gorgeous scouring, fork in the road opening by laser-wielding idols. 20 full skeletons. Most sacred shrine. Star-filled, the guitar sadly soothing inside hours, growls a new devil, and whistle through the pines. Red animal print carpeting for sun worshipers, windows from which to see unsuspecting masters.

SELF-PORTRAIT AS DEATH

for Dom

Maybe I like this Grim Reaper mask
and I won't take it off because I must
go about my business of harvesting
souls and wheat. I feel impelled
to dance on the head of a pin
because I am also an angel,
wearing flowing silk and swaying
like a willow, some illuminated squid-Isadora
Duncan devotee; skull tucked
into the black fold of my cloak
like the frozen clitoris
of an early woman perfectly
preserved in Himalayan ice.
My eyeless interpretive dance
stuttering with my gasoline-pigeon wings
to stay upright on this pin,
this wildly bent dance floor
upon which, I survey gracefully
in my half-levitation,
all that must be destroyed.

THE BHAGAVAD GITA

My rib cage is shattered
and now my heart can easily be removed.
I am peeling away my skull
like an orange to free up my brain.

I place them in the ring together
and maybe instead of fighting
my brain will turn into a gorged phallus
and fuck the brains out of my heart.

THE DEVIL'S CHARIOT

Cloud of gravel dust
blown east.
Sun. Clouds.
No longer in control
I thirst for your mythology
crawling in the desert
in an old movie.
You are a burning
prairie in my heart.
I feel lost, cut open
at the helm of a tumbleweed
or as they call it in Hungarian,
The Devil's Chariot.
The reel is finished and slapping the projector
like a dog chasing its own tail
and what is left
is the white rectangle on the wall,
the forensic misery of the soul
like a paper airplane
launched in a place with no ground
only the weight of itself
victim of perpetual sculpture
no planet's core to return to.
In the alphabet of the body
it is the silence
that holds your shocking vocabulary
at the altar of vertical blood
the hypnosis of the sea
by the moon
that sway of the dock of your bed
the ghost-lit rectangle
with no entrance

like a cathedral of lightning
the osmosis of bone light
chandelier moon-tongue of highway
sliding through the fish eye
watering the mirror threshold of the trees
levitating above the water
cries of the hawk
like needle holes
to string the skulls
for the garland of clouds.
The winter is bringing
the Great Surrounding
the White Rectangle
in the ground
simmer of snowing ash
at the white sand beach of cremation
fenced by living walls of black earth
the open mouth of a toothless river god
that says *you must live without her.*

FIRST TIME

The university tore down the building
I lost my virginity in.
That's how bad it was.

Girls Dorm.
Late. Even the candle is dark.
I am still in love with someone else.
My first love,
like a mosquito
preserved for 46 million years
in honey-colored amber,
full of useless blood.
Can't even clone a dinosaur.

Part not my emerald night gown
with the Spider-Vac
from the Sky Mall.
I'm waiting for marriage.

Oh mustard fields of the damned
consume me like chicken pox.
Shuck me into wallpaper.
3D printed-banana phallus
blossom white toward
the peeling ceiling.
String me up! Empty
clothesline crucifixion!
Everyone is watching!
Cinder block cage fight!

Box-spring twin bed
like a pioneer wagon

full of sleeping children
about to fall of a cliff
due to loss of wheel.

Grocery store. 5AM.
For non-lubricated condoms
that come in a red box.
Trojan Horse salivating.
Hovering solitary
at the locked gate of the castle.
Waiting to be brought inside,
full of sleepless men
with drawn shivering swords
with the whites of their eyes
like eggs in a nest.
Easy prey.

We stay up until 8AM.
After an extra large coffee
from the Amoco Station
I go straight to class
to edit the final draft
of my essay called:

"The way my first love,
kissed me laying on top of me
on the shores of Lake Michigan
in a hot midnight tropical Chicago,
dream blood racing electric
like underwater Fourth of July
snorkel-fetish make out picnic,
with wild coral mountain hair,
69ing stethoscopes and the warm drums
of the eternal mermaid ballet,
ruined everything."

HOWLING F-HOLES

Wounded by swordfish
when I hear the violins
ripping through the vacuum
you created when I left you.
Now I am a captive-bred clone,
an aquarium dweller, kissing
the dark glass falling away
like a silk robe.
Hourglass hissing in the heart,
that hidden ravine,
humming pulley system of blood,
gondola disappearing
into the fog of the mountain
as the tides moves
in and out. Every part of me
is rebuilt over and over
but the memory of you
cannot be updated, replaced
or deleted, like the f-holes
of a violin your absence
is the howling of a song
as old as the wind.

SPIT SHINE

I am walking in the street.
The yellow part of the white
streetlight pavement is domed
with the pitch black hemisphere of God.
The stars provide the peep show,
the voyeuristic jaw into the eye of God,
into the real levitation
the kind where your body fills with heat
the stigmata threshold of pleasure and pain
the concentrated vein intake
of airplane stomach
of love letter ink
of convertible sunlight.

Jacuzzi blood flash-floods across
the entire linoleum body of God.

I am walking in the street
inside of a glass paperweight.
The streetlights make the sphere
fluorescent with quietness
like eighteen inches of snow
on a dark winter morning.
I can hear my shoes in my body.
I can feel the cat in the shadows,
vocabulary bending into fish hooks,
an alien time-freeze dimension,
the white rag of solitude
stretched taut into the reality
of something as convincing as my car keys,
the gentle clockwise release of the lock
the handle dislocating the shoulder
of the door from its socket.

Inside I needed to scream.
I turned the volume up past twenty
and my breath turned into a flash-flood
organ solo as I drove away.

The stoplight by her apartment,
a bright green black hole
I had to hang a right against
the marrowed gravity of the past,
the dark cavities that I loved to sleep in
the dual toothbrush dance in the mirror
the clothes swapping and sweating.

You can see the desperation
of sole devotion to the organ in my eyes
trills in my fingertips, elbows tense,
crashing down the blues scale
the short run up the keys snapping into
to the moment of release,
the double helix tunnel twisting
of the orange snake of blue incense smoke
in my eyes, tearing and blurring
as I watch the entire stick burn.

About to sing, about to cry
about to polish the right shoe of solitude
with my spit, until I can see
the black reflection of my face
staring back at me with bloodshot eyes,
the ash of jazz, in streaks,
across my forehead.

IN THE LIKENESS OF AN EAGLE

It's the temperature as a blade
used to remove the bone
that holds the song hostage
in the solar plexus. The burning
in the muscles where white feathers attach
to your back like a blanket of fish hooks.
Your arms, sore from soaring,
with a yellow eye always
on the river.

Minus 8
Minus 11
Minus 17

The great locus of zero
surrounded by hovering sticks
to keep the babies warm in the trees.
Invisible arcs of black wind in black fields
are made by the blindfolded painter
who has reached a point
where his training can no longer guide him.
The paint must be launched hard,
thrown against the wall
with the entire weight of the body.

More like a samurai than an artist.
More like a train through a sleeping town.
More of a sound than a color.

A weight you can feel deeply,
carrying your groceries to the car.

HANGNAIL

In the darkroom reeling negatives
in pitch blackness
I have a recurring daymare
that involuntarily, I reach down
and rip the hangnail on my right toe
attached to a narrow strip of skin and pull
from its gray nest of dead flesh
like a neon white jet stream
or that thin side-line band
of unlifted masking tape from a mispull,
1/8th of the pus-white inch
straight up over the skull of my kneecap
ripping across the rib cage, over the right cheek
and out the top of my head
like the opening of a FedEx package.

This is something to pay attention to
like a twilit jet stream
threading its orange wake
through the clouds and cloud breaks
dissolving itself as the jet burrows
its tight windshield onward,

my recurrent tinge
my slow slash up the spine
the kind of pain that results
in a higher state of consciousness,
being hung from my thumbs
glass rod broken in my penis
being nailed to a cross
or a Volkswagen
unwrapping the deepest shame

heated didgeridoo blood, droning
like a steaming can of cat food.

While my eyes try to adjust to the dark
in a small room of unbounded blackness
frantically focusing and unfocusing
flashing on the further darkness,

the blinking red bulbs start alternating
in their silent on and offing
and the cold clanger in the bell shield
pendulates like a piston
in its iron woodpecker engine,
a tiny motor starts thinking
and the red and white train gates
come creaking down the hierarchy
and the moon appears on the horizon
while the Amtrak train of the dead
heaves by, rumbling on sparking rails
carrying my entire life
like a glowing film strip.

ROBOT SISYPHUS AND THE SCREAMS OF THE SLAUGHTERHOUSE

for Mom

In bright orange,
on an orange roller coaster,
riding its almost vertical
drop like an erotic urge,
the elevator plummeting
to the ground floor
of the crotch.

In a used bookstore my mother told me
that in the Native American tradition
the bald eagle is a divine messenger.

She bought a nonfiction love story
about the son of an American fighter pilot
and the daughter of a World War II
Japanese fighter pilot
who ending up getting married.

It was a *buy one get one free*
as long as it comes from upstairs
special.
I picked out the largest,
heaviest book I could find
The Audubon Society Encyclopedia of North American Birds
with a screaming bald eagle
on the cover.

The fierce expression on the face of a bald eagle
belies the bird's true nature, for
North America's most celebrated bird

of prey is primarily an eater of fish
and is not above eating any dead fish it finds
along the shores of lakes and rivers.

That's when my mother told me about
walking around the reservoir with Billy
talking about their impending marriage
and a *Haliaeetus Leucocephalus*
a bald eagle,
a bird that is usually only seen by a river
and hardly ever seen in Fairfield, Iowa
appeared out of the trees,
flew in a circle around them
and went back to where is came from,

sharp,
      terrifying,
           and direct,

the path of the roller coaster. . .

Gastronomic lurch at the end
to remind you that you're are exactly
where you began,
and that the hour-plus wait
that you have recently endured
like a cow being prodded
through a nervous line
towards the small doors
of a slaughterhouse
is gone in one minute
of spine compression and winter wind,
a tearjerker-fling
with a crooked infinity.
Unsuccessful uroboros,

Robot Sisyphus and the screams
of a slaughterhouse.

And don't forget after it is over
to buy the picture of the two of us
on the last vertical flipping off
the automatic camera
screaming with open mouths
like eagles.

READY FOR THE BIG TIME

for Eric

Sometimes everything makes sense.
Nexus overlap of singing circles
in the zodiac ballet.

The haunted wildness of the train,
rails bending in xerox light,
searing arc of the satellite.

Cattle brand heartache
with Egyptian cat wings.
Knife emblem blossoming

smoking intricate loneliness.
Not passionate, persistent.
Not desperate, intimately practiced

half ecstatic
in a *Ready for the Big Time* T-shirt
Eno's *Music For Airports* is on.

Drones of ceiling fans,
drones of airplanes and typing,
drones of trains, wind, cars.

Like the 6th Avenue
traffic orchestra sound acting
for Cage smiling,

drone of desire itself,
ironically like a companion.
A parallel demon of pure light.

Shadow of the soul on the wall,
hissing scissoring near
the shrub of self-healing;

now it's a giraffe
now it's a family of ducks
now it's a man no one recognizes

Arms of leaves like photographs
of waterfalls, by waterfalls. Water falls
and in falling, leaves raining.

The bridal shower.
The digesting apple pie.
Ice sculpture at the altar

brought in through the throat
to affix at the burning dime
of the solar plexus.

Blind sungazers
at the last gas station before the interstate
overrun by crows and wild grasses

with snakes the shape of wind
under the skin, around
the monoliths of rubber ribs

of a decomposing whale
clawing through thick clouds
like mountains,

some *real life TV*
commercial for a 1-800 lawyer
selling personal injury options

to the mourning families,
where one or more members
has *accidentally attained Nirvana.*

DRACULA

This is business class, midnight.
His tray table is up.
He is in a hospital-
white three piece suit.
Soft socks over his socks,
free little toothbrush.
He pulls a dark wool blanket
over the narrow rectangle
of his gray recliner;
long fingernails.

The small window
half-reflects his blue face
in glowing bean fields.
In his chest is
the burden of immortality,
the excruciating pressure
of a bag of complimentary peanuts,
a letter unopened,
flat against his heart,
the soothing hum
of the airplane.

The reading light is off
and the Herzog movie
Aguirre the Wrath of God is playing,
soft splashes of light
flickering in the air conditioning
as an indigenous village
is attacked and burnt down;
green bananas and fire.

The temperature drops one degree
and his skin softens.
A giant ship is carried
across a mountain
as he shifts positions.
Now with headphones on, listening
to the swollen river,
the jungle rapids,
looking through his window,
through the lens of a camera
into the yellow butterfly light.

In a grocery store parking lot
a man is being barked at
by a tiny and ravenous dog,
curly white fur and half a face
smashed smooth into the paralysis
of the furthest wedge
in the rear windshield,
as close as it possibly could be.
An electric faucet of madness,
spring-loaded and tense, screaming,
emphatic, foaming at the mouth
like a prophet in the fragile rage
of absolute necessity.
A glass shattering tantrum,
Kinski locked in the bathroom
for forty eight hours
smashing even the toilet bowl
to pearl dust.
This dog knows something.
This dog is Jesus on the cross.

LITTLE LAMB

The clock tower tolls its bell jam.
Thrust-shiver. Blade of the knife
I know you. Waiting for the sedative
of knowledge to wear off.
The cobra is coming out
of the faucet Rikki-Tikki-Tavi!
The telephone is ringing
because I want so badly to hear
your lamb donkey my manger.
I want you to lick me,
the mist from your kiss-spit
to form a cloud
that does not obscure the moon
but rather walks like a lamb
and lies down inside my ear
to take shelter from the cold
near the hunting lodge fire
in my brain stem.
Taxidermy Godhead
on the wall...
Lest ye should forget
the magnitude of my love
o' sweet Lily!
The allure of your cartography
like the hovering circle of Rome
all the intricate lacework
of streets like a snowflake
zoomed out cross-section
of an animal cell,
your blinding white underpants
like a stained glass dove
on the sun.

RAPTURE

It just hits!
When you are pacing
around your apartment
putting things back together
vacuuming, rearranging
your brains and your space
for more incredible activities
like lying on the couch.

You get this feeling of butterflies
in your stomach
and you know exactly what is happening
It's on the verge of being
EROTIC!

You walk quickly
with new determination
you open the door
pull down your pants
sit on the toilet
and the most graceful
thing happens.

Your spine curves in
your head arches back
your mouth opens
you could sing the praise
of the Lord
right there
on the Duchampmobile
it feels so good
your stomach clears its cache

in one luxurious movement
like a ballerina
lifting her arm
at the end
of a dance.

SILVER SPRINGS

Not Frostburg, Maryland!
That's where the Christians
with the loose screw
percussion troupe
are rebuilding the Ark
with no sense of irony.
An actual boat to transport
zoo animals, pets
and suburban housewives
in case the end
of the Mayan Baktun
on Dec 21st is more intense
than we can imagine.

No. Not Frostburg! The swimming
pool in Silver Springs, when I was
13 and masturbation had become
a wild and ecstatic religion
before I was even capable
of producing cum,
finding the water jets
in the deep end
like the warm mouth
of an invisible mermaid.
Some teen heaven.
Some waking dream
about the Great Flood.

PROOF

After Beethoven moonlight,
lunch your legs of Giza
into tandem dive-sky contraction!
Silk kiss throttle two
Christ your holy triangle
and tangle jungles. We
is now parenthetical
since I river feet heads
and you hands me sans me.
Holy reverse-mermaid eyes.
Breasts behind bras,
belly ballet. Valet parked
your heart in my
wolf-box

FLYING MACHINE

Intimate oil of the door-lit floor.
The love of fireflies
and wine. Dog hair in the salad.
Kisses in the furniture.
Erotic tools cut-mouthed
In the heart valves.
Silent water rising, tied up and
chained in the cave.
Oh egg of the brain
laid in a nest of mint
in the garden drinking.
Moonlight from the leaves
build darkness
with telepathy
which you do on my desk.
Your black heels
dig into my thighs
as you sit with advanced mathematics
in my lap like a carburetor
for da Vinci's flying machine,
model of the spine hanging
in the window of the chiropractor's office.
The willpower of the aloe plant.
Leaves born within leaves.
Your teeth bite my tongue
as the pencils rattle in the mason jar
and your legs pour into the floor
like waterfalls, ribbons of silk,
against the mountain.

THE ART OF WAR

The courage to unleash
the quiver shivering full
of arrows. Skeleton blueprint
of the cathedral ceiling
where sewn golden
the hawk domain is
a burning school
of fish, spasm, jerk-kick.
The muscle of the collective.
Brain-flex rainstorm,
avatar of Cupid.
Mobile tilt-steering adjusting
so the target dissolves
and what remains
is just the microscopic hummingbird moves
of a ceiling of hissing arrows,
a white noise drone
mid-flight cloud puppet shape maneuver
dark hammered flat
like a sting ray
like Michael Jackson's glove
like paper covers rock.
It's curtains,
curtains I tell ya.
End of days interior design strategies,
the paint, ladder. . .
and now that you've got control
of the nine iron,
it's time to work
on your short game.

DINNER THEATER OF THE DAMNED

The wound glitching
like the memory of the sword.
Soil crawling with worms.
The blade of the constellation
casting the night sky against the diamond grill,
the Big Dipper, that cast-iron skillet
of the void, those claws on the bath tub,
bite marks on the neck.
I can't tell if this is a murder scene
or the erotic dinner theater of the damned.
Meat detaching from bone,
Crimson cactus flower blooming
like conjoined twins,
oh mirror maker!
Wild Hubble Telescope pixel
crawling with bacteria, stew simmering
with the electric spine of lamb.
Campfire divine. Star farmers.
Illuminated tractors in the sky
combing through the darkness
of your hair,
fingers made of hissing sand
the way the shape of the wind
is half-invisible,
the soundtrack of an open mouth
like a vacuum cleaner
fixing its dentist-grade flood light
on its path of purification
the offering carried by smoke to the gods
levitating fire offerings.
Oh spoon for the baby food!
Oh fork for the leg of pterodactyl!

Oh knife for the warm slab!
The hog champion
atop His throne of slop.
Hairy pink abundance of fluorescent heaven,
the drone of the bug zapper
the percussive death flight
into the light, into
the light, into the light
that hypnosis of a better life
twisted promise of an afterlife.
Rapunzel-motif at the clock tower
dark braided horse-tail of the naked goddess
light years long, muscles tensing for the climb
that long pull into the origin,
ontological aphrodisiac,
like a night swim in a nightmare
aerobic prostrated vertical in devotion
the braid as thick as a forearm
the strong smell of coconut Suave shampoo.

BIG DIPPER
PART II

Shimmy up the balcony
with a dark red rose
in between my teeth.

You can throw your
grappling hooks around
my full frontal nudity.

You can love me like
a Catholic Bible
on a solid oak bookshelf.

You can love me like
a tennis ball rally against
a dark green backboard.

You can love me like
a gleaming wave against
a crooked cliff face.

Rain dark hair.
Pearls and prisms.
Tears and sweat.

The Big Dipper
pouring engine oil
down the back of the night.

"PLEASANT DREAMS"

Is it the fairy in phosphorescent lingerie
serving you steaming muffins in bed tomorrow morning,
her wings tapping up against the white blinds
as she bends over to pour the orange juice?

An orange leaf that turns into a hammock,
the solar netting of monarch butterflies
that hold your weight, while you rock gently
between two prominent trees of your childhood?

Does it include the dark movie theater
version of the history of the future,
the witness, equally the participant,
that welcomes the modestly dressed premonition

that comes as calmly as a glass of milk
on the oak dining room table
in Holden Massachusetts at six PM.
The unabridged dictionary open
on the shelf under the giant windows?

I guess tonight she wanted to save me
from murdering my brother with a golden spear,
then having to outrun the green panther
whose heavy breath is scratching the back
of my neck like an ice storm,

whose head turns into the pyramid
that I am building. Lashes across my back,
and the pharaoh's fat face tattooed
onto my sunburned chest with blue-black
ink that is still wet.

DREAM WITHIN A DREAM

The groaning of the machine
as it wakes up as an industrial
metacognitive metaphor for
the brain before coffee
as it opens its rusted blossom,
chandelier of thrift store knives
like a prom corsage
in need of a good oiling,
or a soapless loofah from the underworld.

Last night you asked me,
"have you ever had a *dream within a dream?*"
not realizing that it was the title
of an Edgar Allan Poe poem
that was quoted by a serial killer
on television after we hung up,
and that now, at Cafe Paradiso
after 3 shots of espresso,
I am half reading
on my smartphone.

I stand amid the roar
Of a surf-tormented shore,
And I hold within my hand
Grains of the golden sand —

"No I have not," I said
trying hard not to reference the movie *Inception*
and feeling some envy when
you said you
had had
a double dream

the other night,
wondering why I seem to be having
the opposite experience,
feeling like Wednesday is unshakable, eternal.
That there nothing except Wednesday.
There is no release. There is no death reward.
No rest. No peace. No dreams.
Just the pelvic bludgeon
of a ceaseless Wednesday.

Is all that we see or seem
But a dream within a dream?

That sea glass factory,
drum solo of driftwood and email
the erotic lifting of the fortune
from the fortune cookie that reads

Sometimes a pat on the back
is just to find the soft spot
for the knife.

LONG EXPOSURE

After a fight with her
you run outside.
Crouching on the sidewalk,
you cry, pull your hair
freezing in your T-shirt
you spit onto the cold street.

Your splotches of spit
on the concrete,
in relationship
to the solitary
fault line and the swoop
of a rubber tire track,
reminds you of a Miro painting.

It is an odd comfort
to be involved in a spontaneous,
slightly delusional,
ekphrastic interaction
with your own accidental
cathartic plagiarism
of surrealist abstraction.

The dark purple of the asphalt
is tinted orange
by the neon WE BUY HOUSES sign
across the street
from the window tinting shop.
A gauntlet is before you
all your wounds
like trained killers
at the tea party of your demise.
The wind makes you shiver.

A distant yellow light makes
a yellow circle on a brick wall.
You remember your first camera
and how you used to float through
the town at night taking pictures
of streetlights and moons
and power plants
piercing the hard gloss
of the coiled negative like a neck
on the chopping block.

Those long exposures after midnight
where even the objects immersed
in darkness start to glow
and the blackness becomes deep and real.
A saturated ink of truth,
halo of drinkable darkness
a 9000 crow black from which
the Iris of the Divine emerges,
like the corpse of a drowned horse.

SELF PORTRAIT WITH ENJAMBMENT

e
  n
  j
  am
  b
  me
  n
  t

FIGURE EIGHT

after Williams "The Great Figure"

Listening to *Fire*
by Hendrix
driving
west on Florida
Avenue I saw
a fire engine's sirens
come toward me
among the reign
of light
as darkness
swallowed the neon city
tomorrow
in the act
of stealing
Williams
fire trucks
and an ambulance
come howling
to a halt
outside my window
across the street
so I reach
to turn off
the light to see
more clearly
then finish
this poem
in the dark
sitting

UNTITLED

A whole tree passed me
on the highway
in a dump truck
and shook the van
like it was an elephant ear leaf
or a water skier
spooning over the wake
like a samurai
jumping onto an enemy horse
at full gallop.

FEAR ITSELF

for Kenzie

"On Valentine's Day
I didn't know what to do.
I found myself in the street
moving, as if by moving
sidewalk, carrying the astronaut silence
with me like a glass of water
until I came across that jazz
inside a black walnut.
You know with ceiling fans
and little UFO lights on the floor,
it was beautiful man.
You know, I was big back in the day!
For the past 27 years I've been
in and out of this town.
There are plenty of other cities
out there for me and we'll see, you know?
When I came back after ten years
it's as if 90 percent of everything beautiful
died or something is missing
that I'm not seeing.
And I believe that! What Maharishi said!
That the CIA was involved
you know what I'm saying?
You can't be here unless
you're going to use this for good,
for the positive.
And the CIA is in the air
like that *fear itself* quote
you know what i mean?
You can't see your own eyes.
There is no autobiography

of an inanimate object,
the Great Pyramid,
not after I cleaned out the filth
and rot in the basement
looking for treasure,
you know what I'm saying,
I actually did that,
with the spiders, and I rescued that piano.
The dust was thick
like the Moon or Arizona man.
And now there is a church
sitting there empty
and nobody is using it.
Nobody needs a building.
He owes me $100,000.
The past four years it feels like
I've been pulling five fire trucks up a mountain
like the strongest man in the universe
competition.
Grunting and sweating
like some sled-dog-Sisyphus,
six fire trucks and a Boeing 747.
And now I can let all that go,
now I can get some coffee
and focus on breathing
and painting, man, that's happening everywhere!
Whatever the next thing is man,
it's beautiful and I feel so much lighter.
You know we're all gonna die
so who really gives a fuck,
you know what I mean?"

INCARNATION PART II

Blown lady on a bike
white hair permanently blown back
like a cement accident.
Pedaling with the dual engines of her desire
some A to B motif.
The whites of her eyes
emblazoned with the evidence
of her serpentine propulsion
through millions of lifetimes
as vampire bats, pythons and black panthers
weaving through the loop
holes of astronomy
in the shadows, rabbits
in a dream of moonlit grass
deer floating in the mist like rishis
lightning of zebras
through the black ink of crows
with yellow hearts
and the secret language of the demon goddess
in a Jurassic mammoth stampede
waking the sleeping gods of earth
in the green cryogenic nudism
of amphibians swimming like astronauts,
robots of biology, slaves
of the cosmic computer
dogs pissing on fire hydrants
signals *turn from green to red*
Chinese checkerboard of birds
the undulating matrix of migration
even the leaves
those transparent ascended masters
of pranayama have hidden agendas.

As I move this pen
there is a suicide of previous consciousness
one small advancement
of a revolution
some twisted wholeness
that imprisons and liberates simultaneously
some psycho synchronicity
a ubiquitous shape shifting freak show
like buckshot for Bambi
an angry school of piranhas
dead set on annihilation.

SWAN PROJECTION

for Patricia

Oh ceaseless torrent
of sex-omniscient! Albino volcano projectile.
White smoke eruption into light.
Swans pouring upwards into clouds
and then raining into mountain lakes divided by zero-
gravity-swimming, thighs, ghost bicycle
running away in a dream, slow
motion seeping forward,
painting a wall of leaves
with the absent square of a movie projector.
Leaves of glass, quilt of arms
holding stone roses with living sap
dripping down the monolith,
stalactite into the void, unblinking
birdbath-eyes reflecting.
The bright yellow talons holding
the bloodshot grapefruits
like robbers stealing the queen's rubies,
silent dancers on the security cameras,
angel-of-death-astronaut clones.
The moment when the wheels touch the runway,
when you kiss the metal nostril,
when the floodwater paints
it's way through the street,
when the telescope traps galaxies
in its see-through petri dish.
Oh Byzantium tadpoles
of the starlit river god, toothless!
Find your bathwater nest of succulents, holy water
and pubic hair woven with silver threads
like a saddle for a medieval horse tightening,

leather straps strong as arms
holding you in place, embroidered.
That dark curve of the eclipse,
the negative space of your legs, twin waterfalls,
as you clench with your pelvis
to stay afloat, half in this world,
as your black horse
enters the black river.

UNTITLED

This has no tone of voice.
This has no body language.
That means that only 7% remains
to communicate with you
and already I have failed.
The gold-sifter's lament,
that constant hissing of sand,
worse than vacation.
In camouflage pajamas
as the forest breathes
opposite you.

INVOLUNTARY BALLET

The ten heads of Ravana reciting
Robert Frost's ten best poems
at the same time
— David Proctor Hurlin

The fundamental driving force
and inspiration of my work,
is actually, in fact, miscommunication.
My true aim is miscommunication.
I am *aiming* to miscommunicate,

pigments to siphon

from and into brain, the overlap
of the inner seascape with the body covered in ash
sitting cross-legged staring into a river.

What I seek to convey in my art,
is the process of miscommunication,
the process of misnumbering pages on purpose.

Equestrian Mondrian!

The process of autographing
life-size posters of Jesus
painted with fair complexion
to look like Patrick
Swayze in Dirty Dancing
holding a baby lamb
with eyes that follow you.

Lake Superior! Mirrors on the ceiling
to tongue the aphrodisiac of melting snow,
shoot the moon and ravish the queen

wearing nothing but her emerald
nightgown, disappearing into the arms
of the forest, to orgasm simultaneously
on a waterbed full of rosewater.

The essence of my work
delves into the issues surrounding how
miscommunication happens,

a radio transmission from the void,
an advertisement for a yard sale
that isn't happening,
a conscious dream through the mouth
of the Durga's *Tyger* into her golden stomach
to burn into ash and bone
and unlearn who I really am.

I consider what steps need to be taken
so that everything remains unclear;

lights,
camera,

with a low voice I say quietly
into a megaphone encased
in a soundproof cube

you have control over
action
alone, not over the fruits.

That's when the tomatoes are unleashed!
Thrown hard in hissing arcs,
like a barrage of arrows.

ASSASSINATION ECSTASY

Built into the blinding green
of the leaves. Psychotic melt
of subjective and objective
double-helixing through skeletons
in some impossible erotic chess feat.
The hanging lights of the ceiling
erect, coming out of the floor
like snakes with light bulb heads.
How are we supposed to hunt and dance
if there is no common ground?
True ground zero is the burning
programmed into all of us,
the terrorists, the children,
the Christmas carolers
with their red mittens,
their machine guns
like water flooding
to the lowest point,
our bodies 99% water,
always searching
for their own ocean-annihilation.
The ascension of the carrot,
pulled electric
from the orange
heart of the earth.
We are born into this world
to be incinerated
and that incineration,
that infinite power of the destroyer
even the sun cannot escape. . .
Perpetual action
of ubiquitous erosion,

black reflection of the void
so deep you can't tell
if you are drinking or being drunken.
Drunk before the throne, beyond
the bones-to-dust explosion
of incarnation.
This is the floorless anti-temple
in which we all pray, alone.
This is where the glass anchor drops
and shatters at the toeless feet
of a consciousness
so brutal,
only It can survive.

HEAVY SNOWSTORM HIT ITS WAY EAST
(ERASURE POEM)

A powerful winter storm
swept across as east
bringing warnings to eastern
and western warnings
for southeast and western
storm stretched south as
where Transportation reported
conditions.

Several highways leaving highways
snow and Information
through east of saying snow
or overwhelm a snow pack
with natural and human-triggered
avalanches.

Storm arriving and departing
at night. That's about
operations of the storm.
The impact of the storm
on its operations elsewhere
across the country.

Portions of
stranding north and south
reopened after numerous were cleared.

The said falling
on the Eastern Plains,
producing some conditions.
for grocery stores,
began the storm.

"They were coming in droves for milk,"
except for non-essential workers in the metro
until 10 AM unless
west of the Kansas parking lot
filling up because
"There's nowhere to go," she said.

Snow totals west of
snow totals mounting
rapidly along the Range
and eastern where inches fell
in 14 inches
in Service
said another foot of
snow the storm moves
out on the snow
at times blowing snow
from the Cities
in the urban corridor from
the south to the north
under a storm.

"The cheese hammered bread of hammered milk,"
said a King at snapping up
A Learjet off a runway
at the Pueblo.
But investigators hadn't determined
if the weather was a factor. None of the 10 people
aboard announced they would be in Denver.

PLAGIARIZING GOD

I am sitting at my typewriter.
I imagine God looking over my shoulder
as I write saying,
Hey I wrote that you asshole.

It feels good to have a constant
companion, a pet monkey
that jumps up and down
with rage when the typewriter
throws the juggling chainsaws
into the ridiculous infinity of air.

I just sit here smiling
with my chapped lips
plagiarizing God,
even if what He wrote sucks!

TINA TURNER OF THE MIND

The components of a bicycle have been squashed into a square block...
—from the description of "Compression" by César from the
20th Century Artbook

Ignorance & illusion Doug with a made
in China spoon and for
k and jack k
nifing pig
truck in the throat
chakra hawk ra
tionale national Tina Turner of the mind the wind George W
ashington's forehead
snapped out parachute
the dim lands of piece hair gunshot
totem bark spark plug
ncural plural geode brain communiqué Jewelius
the muse handcuffed and unconscious in the trunk
of Lorca's A.utomobile-Caldermatology grafted
beaver eyelids
to see (Piet)a Mondrian underwater, floating
Violas-
cension
just be
fore you die the Utah
river fish seam
like a waterfall of stars in a welder helmet
Jesus tryst of the mouth south
urn gospel KKKeats
to quell mi(sp?)ell dezire
of the ankles pyre fire
adorned with silver bells
sliver of ancient light

indicating the unknown,
the silently revolving prize risen
behind door number 5. IV
oui (Uni)verse? of IIIowa
transparent tunnel of eel juice
two the arms of the twitching one
fed to bed
throat rope spelunking
North Pole vaulting
frog mind
peep song zuende
son
on
cross-
town traffic the Burden of Volkswagen
stigmatajive
hand Olivia Newton Baptist Travolta Super Clean
palmistry pilot pie tattva Rabindranothing
Amelia Ophelia
B,uckminster Full,ermuda Hamlet
Benedict.

a facsimile frog
gets thrown into
an old pond

•

a tadpole is dumped
into an old pond
by a school teacher

•

a tree frog falls
into an old pond
by accident

•

old pond
a macro nature photographer
slips and falls in

•

old pond
touch the butt of a frog
splash!

•

a Japanese business man
who had frog legs for dinner
goes skinny dipping

•

a man in a frog suit
decides to reenact
a famous haiku

•

old pond
a handsome young prince
does a belly flop

•

old pond
an early Triassic frog
has not learned to jump

NUDE IN A SNOWSUIT

Run through the fresh snow
with an image of Marcel
pressurized like a gardenia
turned brown with pipe smoke
somewhere in the middle
of the 1269 page Bible
of your heart.

Run through the deep snow
like a unicyclist in
a teeter fight with balance
because of a hay fever sneeze
as two lions roar at the sun
and the noon bell claps
from an absent clock tower.

UNTITLED

Bicycle tires press
to the white pavement
like yellow transparent
leaves made of sunlight
smoothed with rain
onto the glass window
of your forehead.

CIRCUS SHITSCAPE CIRCADIAN

Shotgun-toting biker-demigod
with a Genghis Khan battle helmet
jumps through a ring of fire
chalked with sparks and fireworks
in a narrow slit of night
horse pupil black
with knife-tilts of white
slashing into everything sacred
hijacker with a switchblade comb
burning hissing arcs
into the giant spaces between bones
extrovert in the moonlight
wet spelunking pillage
to the furthest fractal
of blood.
Time reversals
in refrigerator light
walking on cold tile.
Sunken buffalo bones
deep in the aquifer
of the heart.
A satellite is lit
in a tower of outer space
as the engine licks white
noise onto the highway
like shoulder paint,
headlights in a blackout
like pouring a glass of milk
across the entire country.

PHOTOS OF HEAVEN

for Emily

Because after sex, coffee
in bed was luxurious and long,
I missed out on the make-hay-
while-the-sun-shines-inspiration
for a poem about a gallery exhibition
of afterlife landscapes
Photos of Heaven
by Ansel Adams.

Because I was more interested
in whipped cream and Emily
in her baby blue nightgown, I lost,
potentially my "greatest work."
I'm glad I retained "Afterlife Landscapes"
and other shard-like fragments that came
in my post-coital rejected download from the divine
but I forgot how we got to heaven
and that was crucial.

I asked Emily and she had forgotten too.
That was the missing link that made it feel
like magical realism
the angels NYU art students
and not actual deities strewn about
the sunny rocks (or clouds?)
à la Renoir's *Bathers*, the painting
that got me so hot when I was a child-
voyeur in mad-heavy art books.

Alas I'm left with my typical absurdism,
chicken-turd-whitewashed-fluorescence
guaranteed to alienate or eliminate
many of my few Instagram followers.

I knew there was going to be some
f/64 large format virtuosity.
Adams, vulture-esque, amongst the levitating
creamy desertscapes of the divine.
But I got my conception of aperture
backwards, such a common mistake.
Even with my degree in photography
it's still hard to remember
that when dealing with aperture
or "how much light gets in"

The bigger the number
the smaller the hole. The smaller
the number the bigger the hole.

So in my lazy state I thought f/64 was a huge hole
capable of blurring out all the angels
in the background
more like a Sugimoto seascape,
an infinite white rectangle of cloud,
more James Turrell than Raphael.
But it's not. It's a tiny hole.

This is where it all falls apart.
With that tiny hole comes
all that signature depth of field
and *detail in the white* of Adams
so even the upward waterfalls and the golden donkey
that carried Mary to the manger
would be sharply in focus.
More like a color-coordinated group iPhone photo
of a winning football team,
than the euphoric minimalism i was hoping for.

In my devolving free-associative self-portrait
as a half-committed poet

unglazed *with rainwater*
beside the white chickens in my backyard,
the smell of burning ditch leaves in the air,
I have half-remembered or invented
the details coming to me now,
What is the light source in heaven?

Light travels in a straight line.
In the camera obscura of your skull
every "thing" is actually upside down
and your brain flips it over.

The saving grace
is that most likely
aperture is irrelevant.
Maybe in Heaven there
are no things available.
Adams forced to make
his first abstract work;
blinding white lightscapes with no details.
Bone-dust deathscapes.
The thick glossy photo paper burning
with the developer acid of the lord
revealing nothing but nothing.
Incessant Kincadian internal glowing
blown out of proportion
by the impossible-to-use enlarger.
There is no darkroom in heaven,
no way to not ruin everything.

When the huge photographs
are finally revealed to the public
in a see-through SoHo gallery
(South of Heaven)
It's our suspicion that they are probably

all upside down, Ansel postmortem,
lacking the brain to flip them over
but we can't really tell,
with no frames and no subjects
hanging on the walls like windows.

Emily and I are there for the free snacks,
white wine and networking opportunities
anyways.

THE MANIFESTO OF SELF-PROMOTION

People write for two primary reasons: to be read and to make money. What an author writes is based on his purpose: to entertain, to instruct, or to affect his readers. How he writes depends upon his character, personality, zest, and capacity. How a man writes reflects what he himself is.

— Isabell Ziegler

The goal of this poem
is to be selected for publication
in the annual anthology,
Best American Poetry
in the year 2006,
as a way to advertise myself
as a professional poet.

I am most interested
in the inclusion
of my biography
in the back of the anthology
which will contain direct quotes
about the inspiration for,
and the origin of this poem,

which came to me
when I was taking a shower
in my apartment above
Larry's Barber Shop,
washing my ass crack
with sandalwood amber shower gel,
thinking about a way
to write sheet music
for the dropping of a grand piano
on the sidewalk
from 12 stories up,

envisioning a the marquee
for a poetry reading
in the Mark Twain Caves
my name in Vegas CAPS LOCK
next to the title of my book

Stick a Flashlight in Your Mouth
While Standing in Front of a Mirror
Alone in the Dark.

In setting a very clear goal
it smells like Dada
in the opposite sense, which I like.

Because the poem is being used
only as a means to propagate my biography
in the back of *Best American Poetry*
which will then consist mostly
of reflections about the poem,
a Möbius strip of self-annihilation
and self-promotion will be created.

With the tremendous boon
of the invention of the printing press
and the significant popularity of
Best American Poetry
edited by David Lehman,
a snowball effect will occur.
Seeds will be sown deep
into the minds of my contemporaries
and the readers of poetry.
My name will grow in power
and I will become known
as a mysterious antipoet
who showers in the dark

and worships Lord Shiva
and strange women.

With the subconscious noise
of mass hysteria I will emerge
a phoenix from a lake of gasoline
set on fire with peacock feathers dipped in butter.
Astrologically speaking, a rebirthed king
a reincarnation of the cow
Charlie Parker played for,
an aShakespearian-Don Juannabe-
Duchampian Duke of Dick.
With the total support of Natural Law,
my saplings will grow
into a forest of redwoods
and the echoes of my name
whispered in the arching branches
will reach so far and wide
that when my first book is finally published
with a picture of me peeing
on a fire hydrant
for its ultra glossy red cover,
it will be a bestseller overnight.

ABOUT THE AUTHOR

David Hurlin is a professional drummer and percussionist. Drummer for Apocalypso Tantric Noise Choir, Soulmath, Elizabeth Moen, Annalibera, and most recently with The Mike Dillon Band, he has toured all over the country and is in high demand, both as a performer and session drummer. He is working on drum performances and collaborations which lean more toward sound art/sculpture and performance art.

David received his BFA in photography and tabla (Hindustani classical music tradition) from Maharishi University, including seven months abroad in India. His photography took him around the United States photographing his favorite poets – James Tate, Charles Wright, Kim Addonizio, and Cole Swenson, to name a few – which deeply informed his reading and writing of poetry. He took graduate poetry workshops in support of his degree and was involved for a decade with the Monday Night Poets led by his mentor, Diane Frank.

David lives in Fairfield, Iowa with his wife Emily, his son Dil, dog Mochi, cat Monarch, African Leopard tortoise Tortellini, 15 chickens, and 3 ducks.

www.ingramcontent.com/pod-product-compliance
Lightning Source LLC
Chambersburg PA
CBHW031853090426
42741CB00005B/469